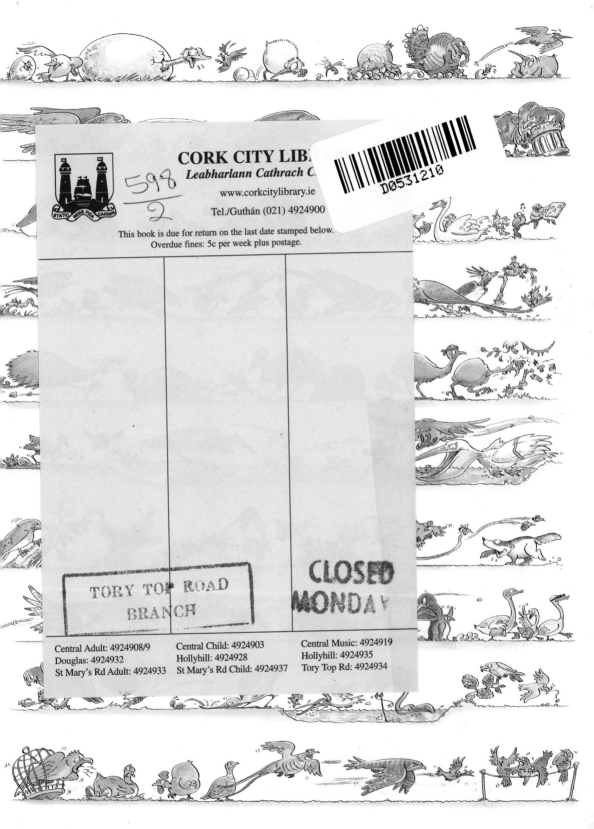

100

things you should know about

BIRDS

100

things you should know about

BIRDS

Jinny Johnson

Consultant: Steve Parker

Miles Kelly
PUBLISHING

First published in 2004 by
Miles Kelly Publishing Ltd
Bardfield Centre, Great Bardfield, Essex, CM7 4SL

2 4 6 8 10 9 7 5 3 1

Publishing Director: Anne Marshall
Project Editor: Neil de Cort
Designer: Sally Lace
Picture Research: Liberty Newton
Proof Reading, Indexing: Janet De Saulles

ISBN 1-84236-347-6

Printed in Singapore

ACKNOWLEDGEMENTS
The Publishers would like to thank the following artists who have
contributed to this book:

Chris Buzer/ Studio Galante
Luca Di Castri/ Studio Galante
Jim Channell/ Bernard Thornton
Illustration
Mike Foster/ Maltings Partnership
L.R. Galante/ Studio Galante
Terry Gabbey/ AFA
Roger Gorringe
Brooks Hagan/ Studio Galante

Alan Harris
Roger Kent
Kevin Maddison
Janos Marffy
Massimiliano Maugeri/ Studio Galante
Eric Robson/ Illustration Limited
Francesco Spadoni/ Studio Galante
Rudi Vizi
Mike White/ Temple Rogers

Cartoons by Mark Davis at Mackerel

www.mileskelly.net
info@mileskelly.net

Contents

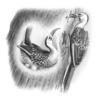

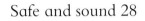

What are birds?

1 **A bird has two legs, a pair of wings and a body that is covered with feathers.** Birds are, perhaps, the animals we see most often in the wild. They live all over the world – everywhere from Antarctica to the hottest deserts and rainforests. They range in size from the huge ostrich, which stands 2.75 metres tall, a whole metre taller than a man, to the tiny bee hummingbird, which is scarcely bigger than a real bee.

Osprey

Greater flamingo

Grey heron

Mallard

Kingfisher

Greater
honeyguide

Helmeted
hornbill

Masai
ostrich

Blue
peafowl

Lesser
green
broadbill

Red-billed
hornbill

African
jacana

Blue-crowned
hanging parrot

The bird world

2 **There are more than 9000 different types, or species, of bird.** These have been organized by scientists into groups called orders which contain many different species. The largest order is called the passerines, also known as perching or song birds. These include common birds such as robins.

Crown

Bill, or beak

Throat

Flight feathers

Light, hollow bones, or skeleton

Kidney

Lung

Heart

Liver

Stomach

Tail feathers

Toes

▲ Most doves and pigeons are hunted by predators. Strong wing muscles, that make up a third of their weight, help them to take off rapidly and accelerate to 80 kilometres an hour.

3 **Birds are the only creatures that have feathers.** The feathers are made of keratin – the same material as our hair and nails. Feathers keep a bird warm and protect it from the wind and rain. Its wing and tail feathers allow a bird to fly. Some birds also have very colourful feathers which help them to attract mates or blend in with their surroundings. This is called camouflage.

▶ The bird with the most feathers is thought to be the whistling swan, with more than 25,000 feathers.

4 **All birds have wings.** These are the bird's front limbs. There are many different wing shapes. Birds that soar in the sky for hours, such as hawks and eagles, have long broad wings. These allow them to make the best use of air currents. Small fast-flying birds such as swifts have slim, pointed wings.

▶ The egg protects the growing young and provides it with food. While the young develops the parent birds, such as this song thrush, keep the egg safe and warm.

5 **All birds lay eggs.** It would be impossible for birds to carry their developing young inside their bodies like mammals do – they would become too heavy to fly.

6 **All birds have a beak for eating.** The beak is made of bone and is covered with a hard material called horn. Birds have different kinds of beak for different types of food. Insect-eating birds tend to have thin, sharp beaks for picking up their tiny prey. The short, strong parrot's beak is ideal for cracking hard-shelled nuts.

◀ Hunting birds, such as this goshawk, have powerful hooked beaks for tearing flesh.

QUIZ

1. How many types of bird are there?
2. How many feathers does the whistling swan have?
3. What are feathers made of?
4. What is the largest order of birds called?
5. What sort of beaks do hunting birds have?

Answers:
5. Powerful hooked beaks
4. The passerines
1. More than 9000 2. More than 25,000 3. Keratin

Big and small

7 **The world's largest bird is the ostrich.** This long-legged bird stands up to 2.75 metres tall and weighs up to 115 kilograms – twice as much as an average adult human. Males are slightly larger than females. The ostrich lives on the grasslands of Africa where it feeds on plant material such as leaves, flowers and seeds.

▼ The great bustard lives in southern Europe and parts of Asia.

8 **The heaviest flying bird is the great bustard.** The male is up to 1 metre long and weighs about 18 kilograms, although the female is slightly smaller. The bustard is a strong flier, but it does spend much of its life on the ground, walking or running on its strong legs.

▼ A bee hummingbird, life size!

9 **The bee hummingbird is the world's smallest bird.** Its body, including its tail, is only about 5 centimetres long and it weighs only 2 grams – about the same as a small spoonful of rice. It lives on Caribbean islands and, like other hummingbirds, feeds on flower nectar.

10 **The largest bird of prey is the Andean condor.** A type of vulture, this bird measures about 110 centimetres long and weighs up to 12 kilograms. This huge bird of prey soars over the Andes Mountains of South America, hunting for food.

▼ Like most vultures, the condor is a scavenger. It looks for carrion, the carcasses of dead animals and the remains of other hunters' kills.

◄ The wandering albatross only comes to land at breeding time. It lays its eggs on islands in the South Pacific, South Atlantic and Indian Ocean.

QUIZ

1. How much does a bee hummingbird weigh?
2. Where do ostriches live?
3. What does the great bustard eat?
4. How long are the wandering albatross's wings?
5. Where does the collared falconet live?

Answers:
1. 2 grams 2. Africa 3. Insects and seeds 4. 3.3 metres from tip to tip 5. India and Southeast Asia

11 **The wandering albatross has the longest wings of any bird.** When outstretched, they measure as much as 3.3 metres from tip to tip. The albatross spends most of its life in the air. It flies over the oceans, searching for fish and squid which it snatches from the water surface.

12 **Wilson's storm petrel is the smallest seabird in the world.** Only 16 to 19 centimetres long, this petrel hops over the water surface snatching up tiny sea creatures to eat. It is very common over the Atlantic, Indian and Antarctic Oceans.

13 **The smallest bird of prey is the collared falconet.** This little bird, which lives in India and Southeast Asia, is only about 19 centimetres long. It hunts insects and other small birds.

Fast movers

14 **The fastest flying bird is the peregrine falcon.** It hunts other birds in the air and makes spectacular high-speed dives to catch its prey. During a hunting dive, a peregrine may move as fast as 180 kilometres an hour. In normal level flight, it flies at about 95 kilometres an hour. Peregrine falcons live almost all over the world.

15 **Ducks and geese are also fast fliers.** Many of them can fly at speeds of more than 65 kilometres an hour. The red-breasted merganser and the common eider duck can fly at up to 100 kilometres an hour.

▼ Sword–billed hummingbird

When this hummingbird lands, it has to tilt its head right back to support the weight of its huge bill.

Tail feathers spread for landing.

16 **A hummingbird's wings beat 50 or more times a second as it hovers in the air.** The tiny bee hummingbird may beat its wings at an amazing 200 times a second. When hovering, the hummingbird holds its body upright and beats its wings backwards and forwards, not up and down, to keep itself in one place in the air. The fast-beating wings make a low buzzing or humming sound that gives these birds their name.

In winter, food can be scarce for birds. You can make your own food cake to help them.

You will need:
225g of suet, lard or dripping
500g of seeds, nuts, biscuit crumbs, cake and other scraps

Ask an adult for help. First melt the fat, and mix it thoroughly with the seed and scraps. Pour it into an old yogurt pot or similar container, and leave it to cool and harden. Remove the cake from the container. Make a hole through the cake, put a string through the hole and hang it from a tree outside.

◀ The peregrine falcon does not just fold its wings and fall like many birds, it actually pushes itself down towards the ground. This powered dive is called a stoop.

17 The swift spends nearly all its life in the air and rarely comes to land. It can catch prey, eat, drink and mate on the wing. After leaving its nest, a young swift may not come to land again for two years, and may fly as far as 500,000 kilometres.

Swifts eat insects which they chase and catch in mid-air!

◀ The spine-tailed swift is thought to fly at speeds of up to 160 kilometres an hour.

Swifts have long, slim wings that are perfect for their life in the air.

18 The greater roadrunner is a fast mover on land. It runs at speeds of 20 kilometres an hour as it hunts for insects, lizards and birds' eggs to eat. It can fly but seems generally to prefer running.

Superb swimmers

19 **Penguins are the best swimmers and divers in the bird world.** They live in and around the Antarctic, which is right at the very south of the world. They spend most of their lives in water, where they catch fish and tiny animals called krill to eat, but they do come to land to breed. Their wings act as strong flippers to push them through the water, and their tail and webbed feet help them steer. Penguins sometimes get around on land by tobogganing over ice on their tummies!

Emperor penguin

20 **The gentoo penguin is one of the fastest swimming birds.** It can swim at up to 27 kilometres an hour – that's faster than most people can run! Mostly, though, penguins probably swim at about 5 to 10 kilometres an hour.

21 The gannet makes an amazing dive from a height of 30 metres above the sea to catch fish in the sea. This seabird spots its prey as it soars above the ocean. Then with wings swept back and neck and beak held straight out in front, the gannet plunges like a dive-bomber. It enters the water, seizes its prey and surfaces a few seconds later.

Northern gannet

QUIZ

1. From how high does a gannet dive?
2. How many kinds of penguin are there?
3. How fast can a gentoo penguin swim?
4. How long can an emperor penguin stay underwater?
5. Where do most kinds of penguin live?

1. 30 metres
2. 18 3. 27 kilometres an hour
4. 18 minutes 5. Antarctica

▼ King penguins and emperor penguins regularly dive deeper than 250 metres. Emperor penguins have been timed making dives lasting more than 18 minutes.

King penguin

◄ There are about 18 different kinds of penguin. Most live in and around Antarctica.

15

Looking good!

22 **At the start of the breeding season male birds try to attract females.** Some do this by showing off their beautiful feathers. Others perform special displays or dances. The male peacock has a long train of colourful feathers. When female birds come near, he begins to spread his tail, showing off the beautiful eye-like markings. He dances up and down and shivers the feathers to get the females' attention.

23 **The male bowerbird attracts a mate by making a structure of twigs called a bower.** The bird spends many hours making it attractive, by decorating it with berries and flowers. Females choose the males with the prettiest bowers. After mating, the female goes away and makes a nest for her eggs. The male's bower is no longer needed.

24 **The male roller performs a special display flight to impress his mate.** Starting high in the air, he tumbles and rolls down to the ground while the female watches from a perch. Rollers are brightly coloured insect-eating birds that live in Africa, Europe, Asia and Australia.

Spotted bowerbird

Fawn breasted bowerbird

Black faced golden bowerbird

◄ Bowerbirds live in Australia and New Guinea.

▼ Female peacocks tend to choose the males with the most attractive feathers.

Cock-of-the-rock

25 **The blue bird of paradise hangs upside-down to show off his wonderful feathers.** As he hangs, his tail feathers spread out and he swings backwards and forwards while making a special call to attract the attention of female birds. Most birds of paradise live in New Guinea. All the males have beautiful plumage, but females are much plainer.

26 **Male cock-of-the-rock dance to attract mates.** Some of the most brightly coloured birds in the world, they gather in groups and leap up and down to show off their plumage to admiring females. They live in the South American rainforest.

27 **The nightingale sings its tuneful song to attract females.** Courtship is the main reason why birds sing, although some may sing at other times of year. A female nightingale chooses a male for his song rather than his looks.

Night birds

28 Some birds, such as the poorwill, hunt insects at night when there is less competition for prey. The poorwill sleeps during the day and wakes up at dusk to start hunting. As it flies, it opens its beak very wide and snaps moths out of the air.

▲ As well as moths, the poorwill also catches grasshoppers and beetles on the ground.

30 The kakapo is the only parrot that is active at night. It is also a ground-living bird. All other parrots are daytime birds that live in and around trees. During the day the kakapo sleeps in a burrow or under a rock, and at night it comes out to find fruit, berries and leaves to eat. It cannot fly, but it can climb up into trees using its beak and feet. The kakapo only lives in New Zealand.

29 The barn owl is perfectly adapted for night-time hunting. Its eyes are very large and sensitive to the dimmest light. Its ears can pinpoint the tiniest sound and help it to locate prey. Most feathers make a sound as they cut through the air, but the fluffy edges of the owl's feathers soften the sound of wing beats so the owl can swoop silently on its prey.

Kakapo

31 Like bats, the oilbird uses sounds to help it fly in darkness. As it flies, it makes clicking noises which bounce off objects in the caves in South America where it lives, and help the bird find its way. At night, the oilbird leaves its cave to feed on the fruits of palm trees.

32 Unlike most birds, the kiwi has a good sense of smell which helps it find food at night. Using the nostrils at the tip of its long beak, the kiwi sniffs out worms and other creatures hiding in the soil. It plunges its beak into the ground to reach its prey.

Kiwi

QUIZ

1. Where are the kiwi's nostrils?
2. Where does the kakapo live?
3. What does the oilbird eat?
4. What's special about the barn owl's feathers?
5. What kind of bird is a poorwill?

1. At the end of its beak
2. New Zealand 3. The fruits of palm trees
4. They have fluffy edges
5. It is a type of nightjar

Home sweet home

33 Birds make nests in which to lay their eggs and keep them safe. The bald eagle makes one of the biggest nests of any bird. The nest is made of sticks and is built in a tall tree or on rocks. It is used year after year. It can grow as large as 2.5 metres across and 3.5 metres deep — big enough for several people to get into!

34 The female hornbill lays her eggs in prison! The male hornbill walls up his mate and her eggs in a tree hole. He blocks the entrance to the hole with mud, leaving only a small opening. The female looks after the eggs and the male brings food, passing it through the opening. Once the eggs hatch the female has to remain safely in the hole with her young for a few weeks while the male supplies food.

▲ The bald eagle lives in North America. In 1782 the United States adopted the bald eagle as its national bird.

The male weaver bird twists strips of leaves around a branch or twig.

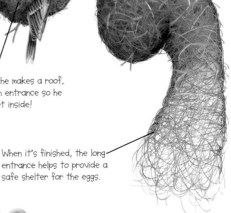

35 The male weaver bird makes a nest from grass and stems.

He knots and weaves the pieces together to make a long nest, which hangs from the branch of a tree. The nest makes a warm, cosy home for the eggs and young, and is also very hard for any predator to get into.

Then, he makes a roof, and an entrance so he can get inside!

When it's finished, the long entrance helps to provide a safe shelter for the eggs.

36 The cave swiftlet makes a nest from its own saliva or spit.

It uses the spit as glue to make a cup-shaped nest of feathers and grass.

37 The mallee fowl makes a temperature-controlled nest mound.

It is made of plants covered with sand. As the plants rot, the inside of the mound gets warmer. The female bird lays her eggs in holes made in the sides of the mound. The male bird then keeps a check on the temperature with his beak. If the mound cools, he adds more sand. If it gets too hot he makes some openings to let warmth out.

Mallee fowl

38 The cuckoo doesn't make a nest at all – she lays her eggs in the nests of other birds!

She lays up to 12 eggs, all in different nests. The owner of the nest is called the host bird. The female cuckoo removes one of the host bird's eggs before she puts one of her own in, so the number in the nest remains the same.

I DON'T BELIEVE IT!

Most birds take several minutes to lay an egg. The cuckoo can lay her egg in 9 seconds! This allows her to pop her egg into a nest while the owner's back is turned.

Great travellers

39 **The Canada goose spends the summer in the Arctic and flies south in winter.** This regular journey is called a migration. In summer, the Arctic bursts into bloom and there are plenty of plants for the geese to eat while they lay their eggs and rear their young. In autumn, when the weather turns cold, they migrate, this means they leave to fly to warmer climates farther south. This means that the bird gets warmer weather all year round.

▼ The Canada goose tends to return to its birthplace to breed.

▶ The Arctic tern travels farther than any other bird and sees more hours of daylight each year than any other creature.

40 **The Arctic tern makes one of the longest migrations of any bird.** It breeds in the Arctic during the northern summer. Then, as the northern winter approaches, the tern makes the long journey south to the Antarctic – a trip of some 15,000 kilometres – where it catches the southern summer. In this way the tern gets the benefit of long daylight hours for feeding all year round.

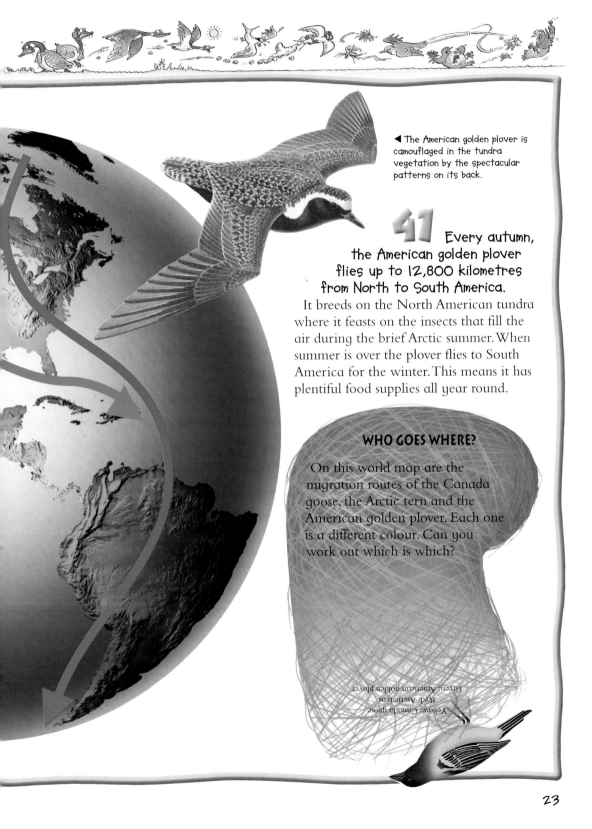

◀ The American golden plover is camouflaged in the tundra vegetation by the spectacular patterns on its back.

41 Every autumn, the American golden plover flies up to 12,800 kilometres from North to South America.

It breeds on the North American tundra where it feasts on the insects that fill the air during the brief Arctic summer. When summer is over the plover flies to South America for the winter. This means it has plentiful food supplies all year round.

WHO GOES WHERE?

On this world map are the migration routes of the Canada goose, the Arctic tern and the American golden plover. Each one is a different colour. Can you work out which is which?

Green: American golden plover.
Red: Arctic tern.
Yellow: Canada goose.

Desert dwellers

42 **Many desert birds have sandy-brown feathers to blend with their surroundings.** This helps them hide from their enemies. The cream-coloured courser lives in desert lands in Africa and parts of Asia. It is hard to see on the ground, but when it flies, the black and white pattern on its wings makes it more obvious. So the courser runs around rather than fly. It feeds on insects and other creatures it digs from the desert sands.

▲ Cream-coloured courser

43 **Birds may have to travel long distances to find water in the desert.** But this is not always possible for little chicks. To solve this problem, the male sandgrouse has special feathers on his tummy which act like sponges to hold water. He flies off to find water and thoroughly soaks his feathers. He then returns home where his young thirstily gulp down the water that he's brought.

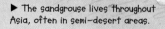

▶ The sandgrouse lives throughout Asia, often in semi-desert areas.

▶ The elf owl is able to catch prey in its feet as it flies.

44 **The elf owl makes its nest in a hole in a desert cactus.** This prickly, uncomfortable home helps to keep the owl's eggs safe from enemies, who do not want to struggle through the cactus' spines. The elf owl is one of the smallest owls in the world and is only about 14 centimetres long. It lives in desert areas in the southwest of the USA.

45

The cactus wren
eats cactus fruits and
berries. This little bird hops
about among the spines of cactus plants
and takes any juicy morsels it can find. It
also catches insects, small lizards and
frogs on the ground. Cactus wrens live in
the southwestern USA.

46

The lappet–faced vulture scavenges for
its food. It glides over the deserts of Africa and the
Middle East, searching for dead animals or the left-overs
of hunters such as lions. When it spots something, the
vulture swoops down and attacks the carcass with its
strong hooked bill. Its head and neck are bare so it
does not have to spend time cleaning its feathers
after feeding from a messy carcass.

▼ The lappet–faced vulture has
very broad wings. These are ideal
for soaring high above the plains of
its African home, searching for food.

Staying safe

47 Birds have clever ways of hiding themselves from enemies. The tawny frogmouth is an Australian bird that hunts at night. During the day, it rests in a tree where its brownish, mottled feathers make it hard to see. If the bird senses danger it stretches itself, with its beak pointing upwards, so that it looks almost exactly like an old broken branch or tree stump.

Tawny frogmouth

48 If a predator comes too close to her nest and young, the female killdeer leads the enemy away by a clever trick. She moves away from the nest, which is made on the ground, making sure the predator has noticed her. She then starts to drag one wing as though she is injured and is easy prey. When she has led the predator far enough away from her young she suddenly flies up into the air and escapes.

▶ The killdeer lives in North America.

49 Guillemots find that there is safety in numbers. Thousands of these birds live together on cliff tops and rocks. They do not build nests but simply lay their eggs on the rock or bare earth. Most land hunters cannot reach the birds on these rocks, and any flying egg thieves are soon driven away by the mass of screeching, pecking birds.

I DON'T BELIEVE IT!

The guillemot's egg is pear-shaped with one end much more pointed than the other. This means that the egg rolls round in a circle if it is pushed or knocked, so does not fall off the cliff.

Safe and sound

50 **A bird's egg protects the developing chick inside.** The yellow yolk in the egg provides the baby bird with food while it is growing. Layers of egg white, called albumen, cushion the chick and keep it warm, while the hard shell keeps everything safe. The shell is porous – it allows air in and out so that the chick can breathe. The parent birds keep the egg warm in a nest. This is called incubation.

1. The chick starts to chip away at the egg.

53 **The kiwi lays an egg a quarter of her own size.** The egg weighs 420 grams – the kiwi only weighs 1.7 kilograms. This is like a new baby weighing 17.5 kilograms, most weigh about 3.5 kilograms.

51 **The biggest egg in the world is laid by the ostrich.** An ostrich egg weighs about 1.5 kilograms – an average hen's egg weighs only about 50 grams. The shell of the ostrich egg is very strong, measuring up to 2 millimetres thick.

52 **The smallest egg in the world is laid by the bee hummingbird.** It weighs about 0.3 grams. The bird itself weighs only 2 grams.

Ostrich egg

Bee hummingbird egg

2. The chick uses its egg tooth to break free.

3. The egg splits wide open.

4. The chick is able to wriggle free. Its parents will look after it for several weeks until it can look after itself.

54 The number of eggs laid in a clutch varies from 1 to more than 20. A clutch is the name for the number of eggs that a bird lays in one go. The number of clutches per year also changes from bird to bird. The grey partridge lays one of the biggest clutches, with an average of 15 to 19 eggs, and the common turkey usually lays 10 to 15 eggs. The emperor penguin lays one egg a year.

▲ Common turkey

QUIZ

1. How thick is the shell of an ostrich egg?
2. How many eggs a year does the emperor penguin lay?
3. How much does the bee hummingbird's egg weigh?
4. For how long does the wandering albatross incubate its eggs?
5. For how long does the great spotted woodpecker incubate its eggs?

1. 2 millimetres 2. One 3. 0.3 grams 4. up to 82 days 5. 10 days

55 The great spotted woodpecker incubates its egg for only 10 days. This is one of the shortest incubation periods of any bird. The longest incubation period is of the wandering albatross, which incubates its eggs for up to 82 days.

Deadly hunters

56 **The golden eagle is one of the fiercest hunters of all birds.** The eagle has extremely keen eyesight and can see objects from a far greater distance than humans can manage. When it spies a victim, the eagle dives down and seizes its prey in its powerful talons. It then rips the flesh apart with its strong hooked beak. The golden eagle usually has two eggs. However, the first chick to hatch often kills the younger chick. Golden eagles live in North America, Europe, North Africa and Asia.

Steller's sea eagle

57 **The sea eagle feeds on fish that it snatches from the water surface.** The eagle soars over the ocean searching for signs of prey. It swoops down, seizes a fish in its sharp claws and flies off to a rock or cliff to eat its meal. Spikes on the soles of the eagle's feet help it hold onto its slippery prey. Other eagles have special prey, too. The snake eagle feeds mostly on snakes and lizards. It has short, rough-surfaced toes that help it grip its prey.

▼ The golden eagle can soar for hours on its huge wings, searching for prey such as rabbits and other birds.

58 **The raven is the biggest of all the songbirds and a powerful hunter.** It grows up to 63 centimetres long, it has a strong, hooked beak for attacking its victims and it can run fast on the ground as well as fly when chasing prey. Rats and mice are its main catches, but it steals other birds' eggs and can even kill a creature as large as a rabbit. Ravens also scavenge for food, taking animals that are already dead or the remains of the kills of other hunters.

▶ Ravens live in North America, Europe, and parts of Africa and Asia.

Caring for the young

59 Emperor penguins have the worst breeding conditions of any bird. They lay eggs and rear their young on the Antarctic ice. The female penguin lays one egg at the start of the Antarctic winter. She returns to the sea, leaving her partner to incubate the egg on his feet. The egg is covered by a flap of the father's skin and feathers – so it is much warmer than the surroundings.

▲ While the male penguin incubates the egg he does not eat. When the chick hatches, the female returns to take over its care while the exhausted, hungry male finds food.

60 Pigeons feed their young on 'pigeon milk'. This special liquid is made in the lining of part of the bird's throat, called the crop. The young birds are fed on this for the first few days of their life and then start to eat seeds and other solid food.

61 Hawks and falcons care for their young and bring them food for many weeks. Their chicks are born blind and helpless. They are totally dependent on their parents for food and protection until they grow large enough to hunt for themselves.

▶ A sparrowhawk and her chicks.

A mallard, a type of duck, with her ducklings.

62 Other birds, such as ducks and geese, are able to run around and find food as soon as they hatch. Baby ducks follow the first moving thing they see when they hatch – usually their mother. This reaction is called imprinting. It is a form of very rapid learning that can happen only in the first few hours of an animal's life. Imprinting ensures that the young birds stay close to their mother and do not wander away.

I DON'T BELIEVE IT!
While male penguins incubate their eggs they huddle together for warmth. The birds take it in turns to stand on the outside and take the force of the freezing winds.

63 Swans carry their young on their back as they swim. This allows the parent bird to move fast without having to wait for the young, called cygnets, to keep up. When the cygnets are riding on the parent bird's back they are safe from enemies.

64 Young birds must learn their songs from adults. A young bird such as a chaffinch is born being able to make sounds. But, like a human baby learning to speak, it has to learn the chaffinch song by listening to its parents and practising.

Deep in the jungle

Harpy eagle

65 **Birds of paradise are among the most colourful of all rainforest birds.** Only the males have brilliant plumage and decorative feathers; the females are generally much plainer. There are about 42 different kinds of birds of paradise and they all live in the rainforests of New Guinea and northeast Australia. Fruit is their main food but some also feed on insects and spiders.

66 **The Congo peafowl was only discovered in 1936.** It lives in the dense rainforest of West Africa and has rarely been seen. The male bird has beautiful glossy feathers while the female is mostly brown and black.

Hoatzin

Congo peafowl

67 **The harpy eagle is the world's largest eagle.** It is about 90 centimetres long and has huge feet and long sharp claws. It feeds on rainforest animals such as monkeys and sloths, which it catches in the trees.

68 **The hoatzin builds its nest overhanging water.** If its chicks are in danger they can escape by dropping into the water and swimming to safety. This strange bird with its ragged crest lives in the Amazon rainforest in South America.

69 The quetzal has magnificent tail feathers which are up to 90 centimetres long. This beautiful bird lives in the rainforests of Central America. It was worshipped as a sacred bird by the ancient Mayan and Aztec people.

Quetzal

Scarlet macaw

Junglefowl

70 The scarlet macaw is one of the largest parrots in the world. This spectacular bird is 85 centimetres long, including its very long tailand lives in the South American rainforest. It moves in flocks of 20 or so that screech loudly as they fly from tree to tree feeding on fruit and leaves.

71 The junglefowl is the ancestor of the farmyard chicken. This colourful bird lives in the Southeast Asian rainforest, where it feeds on seeds and insects.

The biggest birds

72 **The fast-running emu is the largest bird in Australia.** Like the ostrich it cannot fly, but it can run at speeds of more than 50 kilometres an hour on its long legs as it searches for fruit, berries and insects to eat. In the breeding season the female lays up to 10 eggs in a dip in the ground. The male then takes over and incubates the clutch.

▼ These flightless birds are among the largest birds in the world.

Emu

Kiwi

▼ The ostrich is the world's fastest two-legged runner. It is specially adapted for speed, and can run at up to 70 kilometres an hour.

Very powerful upper leg muscles

Extra flexible knees

Long, strong legs

Bendy two-toed feet

73 The rhea lives on the grassy plains of South America. It is a fast-running bird but it cannot fly. It eats mainly grass and other small plants, but it also catches insects and other small creatures such as lizards. In the breeding season, male rheas fight to gather a flock of females. Once he has his flock, the male rhea digs a nest in the ground. Each of the females lays her eggs in this nest. The male incubates the eggs, and he looks after the chicks until they are about six months old.

▼ The rhea can sprint faster than a horse, reaching speeds of up to 50 kilometres an hour.

Cassowary

74 Cassowaries are flightless birds which live in the rainforests of Australia and New Guinea. There are three species – all are large birds with long, strong legs and big, sharp-clawed feet. On the cassowary's head is a large horny crest, called a casque. Experts think that when the bird is moving through the dense forest, it holds its head down and uses the casque to help it break its way through the tangle of plants.

I DON'T BELIEVE IT!

One rhea egg is the equivalent to about 12 hen's eggs. It has long been a tasty feast for local people.

Messing about in the river

75 **The jacana can walk on water!**
It has amazingly long toes that spread the bird's weight over a large area and allow it to walk on floating lily pads as it hunts for food such as insects and seeds. Jacanas can also swim and dive. There are eight different types of jacana, also called lilytrotters. They live in parts of North and South America, Africa and Asia.

76 **The kingfisher makes its nest in a tunnel in a riverbank.**
Using their strong beaks, a male and female pair dig a tunnel up to 60 centimetres long and make a nesting chamber at the end. The female lays up to eight eggs which both parents take turns to look after.

77 **The heron catches fish and other water creatures.**
This long-legged bird stands on the shore or in shallow water and reaches forward to grab its prey with a swift thrust of its dagger-like beak.

78 A small bird called the dipper is well–adapted to river life. It usually lives around fast-flowing streams and can swim and dive well. It can even walk along the bottom of a stream, snapping up prey such as insects and other small creatures. There are five different types of dipper and they live in North and South America, Asia and Europe.

QUIZ

1. How long is a kingfisher's nest burrow?
2. How many types of jacana are there?
3. What is the osprey's prey?
4. What helps the osprey hold onto its prey?
5. What do pelicans eat?

1. About 60 centimetres 2. Eight 3. Fish 4. Spikes on the soles of its feet 5. Fish

79 The pelican collects fish in the big pouch that hangs beneath its long beak. When the pelican pushes its beak into the water the pouch stretches and fills with water – and fish. When the pelican then lifts its head up, the water drains out of the pouch leaving any food behind.

The pelican uses its pouch like a net to catch fish.

80 The osprey is a bird of prey which feeds mainly on fish. This bird is found nearly all over the world near rivers and lakes. It watches for prey from the air then plunges into the water with its feet held out in front ready to grab a fish. Special spikes on the soles of its feet help it hold onto its slippery catch.

39

Can I have some more?

81 The woodpecker uses its special strong beak to bore into tree trunks and catch insects. The bird holds on tightly to a tree trunk with the help of its strong feet and sharp claws. Its stiff tail feathers also help to give it support. It starts to hammer into the trunk, disturbing wood-boring insects that live beneath the tree bark. The insects try to flee, but the woodpecker quickly snaps them up.

▶ There are more than 200 different kinds of woodpecker, including this Eurasian woodpecker. They live in North and South America, Africa, Europe and Asia.

82 **The antbird keeps watch over army ants as they march through the forest.** The bird flies just ahead of the ants and perches on a low branch. It then pounces on the many insects, spiders and other small creatures that try to escape from the marching column of ants. Some antbirds also eat the ants themselves. There are about 240 different types of antbirds that live in Central and South America.

▼ Honeyguides have been known to lead honey-loving humans to bees' nests.

84 **The honeyguide bird uses the honey badger to help it get food.** The honeyguide feeds on bee grubs and honey. It can find the bees' nests but it is not strong enough to break into them. So it looks for the honey badger to help. It leads the badger toward the bees' nest. When the honey badger smashes into the nest, the honeyguide can also eat its fill.

83 **The hummingbird feeds on flower nectar.** Nectar is a sweet liquid made by flowers to attract pollinating insects. It is not always easy for birds to reach, but the hummingbird is able to hover in front of the flower while it sips the nectar using its long tongue.

I DON'T BELIEVE IT!

The hummingbird has to eat lots of nectar to get enough energy to survive. If a human were to work as hard as a hummingbird, he or she would need to eat three times their weight in potatoes each day.

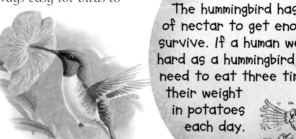

Life in snow and ice

85 The coldest places on Earth are the Arctic and the Antarctic. The Arctic is as far north as it is possible to go, and the Antarctic is south, at the bottom of the Earth. The snowy owl is one of the largest birds in the Arctic. Its white feathers hide it in the snow

86 The snow bunting breeds on Arctic islands and farther north than any other bird. The female makes a nest of grasses, moss and lichens on the ground. She lays four to eight eggs and, when they hatch, both parents help to care for the young. Seeds, buds and insects are the snow bunting's main foods.

88 Sheathbills scavenge any food they can find. These large white birds live in the far south on islands close to the Antarctic. They do catch fish but they also search the beaches for any dead animals they can eat. They also snatch weak or dying young from seals and penguins.

Snowy sheathbill

Snow bunting

Snowy owl

Ptarmigan

87 The ptarmigan has white feathers in the winter to help it hide from enemies among the winter snows in the Arctic. But in summer its white plumage would make it very obvious, so the ptarmigan moults and grows brown and grey feathers.

89 Penguins have a thick layer of fat just under their skin to help protect them from the cold. Their feathers are waterproof and very tightly packed for warmth. Penguins live mainly in Antarctica, but some live in South Africa, South America and Australia.

QUIZ

All of these birds live in snow and ice, but some of them live in the north and some live in the south. Can you tell which live in the north, the Arctic, and which live in the south, the Antarctic?

All belong in the north, the Arctic, except for the penguins and the snowy sheathbill which belong in the south, the Antarctic.

Emperor penguin

90 The tundra swan lays its eggs and rears its young in the tundra of the Arctic. The female bird makes a nest on the ground and lays up to five eggs. Both male and female care for the young. In autumn the whole family migrates, travels south to spend the winter in warmer lands.

Tundra swan

43

Special beaks

91 The snail kite feeds only on water snails and its long upper beak is specially shaped for this strange diet. When the kite catches a snail, it holds it in one foot while standing on a branch or other perch. It strikes the snail's body with its sharp beak and shakes it from the shell.

◄ The snail kite lives in the southern USA, and Central and South America, but it is now very rare.

Toco toucan

92 The toco toucan's colourful beak is about 19 centimetres long. It allows the toucan to pick fruit and berries at the end of branches that it would not otherwise be able to reach. There are more than 40 different kinds of toucan, and all have large beaks of different colours. The colours and patterns may help the birds attract mates.

93 The wrybill is the only bird with a beak that curves to the right. The wrybill is a type of plover which lives in New Zealand. It sweeps its beak over the ground in circles to pick up insects.

Black skimmer

94 The lower half of the skimmer's beak is longer than the upper half. This allows it to catch fish in a special way. The skimmer flies just above the water with the lower part of its beak below the surface. When it comes across a fish, the skimmer snaps the upper part of its beak down to trap the prey.

I DON'T BELIEVE IT!

The flamingo's legs may look as if they are back to front. In fact, what appear to be the bird's knees are really its ankles!

96 The crossbill has a very unusual beak which crosses at the tip. The shape of this beak allows the bird to open out the scales of pine cones and remove the seeds it feeds on.

95 The flamingo uses its beak to filter food from shallow water. It stands in the water with its head down and its beak beneath the surface. Water flows into the beak and is pushed out again by the flamingo's large tongue. Any tiny creatures such as insects and shellfish are trapped on bristles in the beak.

Birds and people

97 **People buying and selling caged birds has led to some species becoming extremely rare.** Some pet birds such as budgerigars are bred in captivity, but others such as parrots are taken from the wild, even though this is now illegal. The beautiful hyacinth macaw, which used to be common in South American jungles, is now rare because of people stealing them from the wild to sell.

Red–fan parrot

King parrot

▲ Hyacinth macaw

98 **In some parts of the world, people still keep falcons for hunting.** The birds are kept in captivity and trained to kill rabbits and other animals, and bring them back to their master. When the birds are taken out hunting, they wear special hoods over their heads. These are removed when the bird is released to chase its prey.

99 **Many kinds of birds are reared for their eggs and meat.** Chickens and their eggs are a major food in many countries, and ducks, geese and turkeys are also eaten. These are all specially domesticated species but some wild birds, such as pheasants, partridge and grouse, are also used as food.

100 Starlings are very common city birds. Huge flocks are often seen gathering to roost, or sleep on buildings. Starlings originally lived in Europe and Asia but have been taken to other countries and been just as successful. For example, 100 years ago 120 starlings were released in New York. Now starlings are among the most common birds in North America. The starling is very adaptable. It will eat a wide range of foods including, insects, seeds and fruits, and will nest almost anywhere.

Starling

I DON'T BELIEVE IT!

In one city crows wait by traffic lights. When the lights are red they place walnuts in front of the cars. When the lights turn green the cars move over the nuts, breaking the shells. The birds then fly down and pick up the kernels!

Index